Mobile Car Detailing Business

Put in a Bit of Elbow Grease and Make Sizeable Profits

Zayne Wascomb

Table of Contents

Introduction

Do you love being around cars? I know that I sure do! The look, the feel, everything about a car is truly something special.

What's even better is getting paid to transform cars and make them look nice and shiny. You might love cars and be looking for a way to get paid to be around cars. You might just need a way to make some extra cash.

Maybe you want to start a business that can allow you to be able to quit your job. Whatever your motivations are for wanting to start this business, just know that you've come to the right place. In this book, I'm going to outline everything you need to know in order to get started with this business. You're going to have the confidence you need to be able to get going and know that you can get customers.

Chapter 1: You Don't Have to Go All Out in Order to Get Started

In this chapter, I want to break down what you're going to need in order to get started with this business. It's not going to be as crazy as you might think! I also want to share with you some of the benefits to starting off your business as a mobile detailer.

Why Mobile Detailing?

When you think of car detailing, what do you typically think of? You might think of going to a physical location that is a car wash and detail spot in the same location. That's great and all, but I believe that going mobile is a much easier and better way to start out. Here are a few reasons why:

Physical Locations are Pricey

Having a physical location is great if it's in a high traffic area. Your business is continuously going to be advertising itself to anyone who drives by it.

The free marketing and exposure can really help out your business.

However, both the marketing and exposure come at a cost. You're going to have to pay rent on that location, and it's going to cost you thousands of dollars every single month, more than likely. I don't know about you, but I would have a hard time getting something like that started. I'd rather get started in an easier way so that I can turn a profit faster.

I don't want to spend my first few months in business breaking my back just to try to break even. By starting off your car detailing business being mobile, you get to avoid those expensive start-up costs that hold a lot of people back from getting started in the first place. Even if you want to start with a physical location like your garage or shop, you still have to consider the logistics of the customer.

Where are they going to wait while you detail their car? Are they going to wait in the garage? I don't like having the customer watch me while I do my work, and you probably don't either.

What if your garage doesn't have air conditioning and it's hot during the summer months? Do you want the person waiting in your home? That definitely seems awkward, to say the least. It really boils down to mobile being the best option. You get to skip on the costs of a physical location, and you don't have to worry about where the customer is going to be if you operate from your own home.

It's More Convenient for the Customer

In the modern age, convenience is king. Do you scroll on social media on your phone or on a desktop? More than likely, you use your phone because it's way easier to pull your phone out of your pocket on your couch than to sit at a clunky desk.

Do you like getting in your car and going through a drive-through, or would you rather have someone else deliver your food to you? Do you like going to the movies, or would you rather watch movies on a streaming service from the comfort of your home? Don't get me wrong, I like going to the movies and drive throughs, but I want you to think about industries that have been born purely because we love convenience.

People can get in their car and go through a drive-through, but it sure is nice to have someone else deliver the food to us, and thus the meal delivery service has been booming in recent times. When it comes to car detailing, things are no different. Would you rather drive to a physical location and have to wait in a lobby for an hour for someone to detail your car?

Or would you rather be at home doing whatever you want and have someone else come to you? The second option sounds way better. At a certain point, I'm going to get tired of waiting around.

I'd almost want them to rush and finish the job so I can go home because I have other things that I want to do. If I'm already at home to begin with, then there's no pressure for the car detailer to finish by a certain time, unless I have somewhere to be. Much like food delivery, you don't have to leave your own home, which is absolutely amazing!

This is far better for the customer, and let's face the facts; it's more so in alignment with what people want in modern times. If something is cheaper to start and what people prefer, then I'm definitely about it!

You Can Get Started Today

Literally, this business is so easy to get up and running, it's not even funny. The start-up costs for this business are super cheap. You likely already have the money you need in order to get started with detailing.

If you don't, then there are plenty of ways that you can get the cash you need because it isn't that much. You can even save for a month or two and be ready to start. If you wanted to start a car detailing business at a physical location, you'd have to search for a location, then go through the process of signing the lease. This is all time that you could spend servicing clients, which is why I like this business so much.

Great Profit Margins

Given the low amount of up-front money needed to start this business, your profit margins are going to be really good. The cost of your ongoing supplies aren't going to be that much either. You'll occasionally need to buy things like more soap or more towels every now and then, but the most expensive things you'll incur will be at the start.

You'll use your first few cars to break even with your initial expenses, but after that, the majority of what you make is profit. Some businesses operate on 10% margins, which is not fun. I can't imagine investing all of this time and money into a business to only make a 10% margin. I'd much rather flip that on its head and make closer to a 90% margin.

Resist the Urge

Now, I want to start to get into what some of these supplies are that you're going to need for your mobile detailing business. If you go online, you might feel intimidated or overwhelmed. This is because you'll see people who are mobile detailers with decked out vans.

They have multiple spray bottles. They have little compartments to hold the spray bottles in. They have multiple different hoses wrapped up in the van and multiple compartments meant specifically for their extractor, pressure washer, and dry vac.

The van also has its own water tank, so everything can be completed from the van and doesn't require use of the customer's outlet or water spout. It's a sight to see, honestly. You might look at something like that and think that this business is costly to get started.

And for a setup like I just described, it definitely would be expensive. First off, you'd have to buy a van for mobile detailing. That's something you likely don't have already, so you'd have to go out and buy one.

By no means is that going to be cheap. Then you're likely going to spend close to $10,000 to get the van fully decked out and set up with all of the different compartments that you need. I'm not saying it isn't worth it, but starting out, I don't think it's necessarily a good idea.

You might not have that kind of up front capital to invest in this kind of setup. Also, think about the number of cars you're going to have to detail just to break even. You're running a business, which means that your number one goal is to make a profit.

Your goal isn't to look cool or feel good about what you're driving around in. Provide value to your customer by doing a good job. That's what people care about.

They're not going to think twice about you being in your personal vehicle. If you see others with these fully decked out setups, it may make you feel like you need to do that same thing, I'm telling you that you don't. Keep in mind that you haven't even sold your first client yet.

What if you go all out for the van and get it fully set up only to realize that you're struggling to land clients? I'd rather spend a few hundred and then come to that realization rather than investing thousands.

As you start to build up your clientele and have some extra money to reinvest, then you can look into getting a van and getting it decked out with all of the different bells and whistles. Until that day comes though, start out lean and mean.

What Will Get You Started?

What are the basics you're going to need to start your very own mobile detailing business? Here's a breakdown of some of the items you'll need:

Pressure Washer

This is the item you'll use to wash the exterior of someone's car. The higher the PSI is on the pressure washer, the more pressure the water will have. I recommend getting a pressure washer with 2,000 PSI, which should run you around $200.

You also want to make sure your pressure washer is electric and not gas. Gas pressure washers are loud and annoying because you'll regularly have to fill them up with gas. Yes, you get the convenience of dealing with less cords, but you're already going to need a water supply anyways, so what does needing an electrical outlet matter? A pressure washer is going to be your single biggest expense to get started, so everything is downhill from here.

Dry Vac

You're going to need a dry vac to suck up any loose debris on the floor of the car, in between the seats, etc. A standard dry vac will be able to get the job done, and you can get one for around $60-$100, depending on the model.

Extractor

You're going to need something that can pull up stains out of cushions and floorboards. The good thing is that small portable extractors really aren't that much. They'll usually cost around $100-$150, depending on what model you get.

They're super easy to use, and it can really enhance your service. Imagine not using an extractor. Sure, you can get the console and dashboard looking good.

You can get rid of any dirt and debris in the car. But if the seats still have big stains on them, the overall look and feel of the car will still seem off. With an extractor, you'll be able to get out stains and really wow the customer with how their vehicle looks after the service.

Garden Hose

You're going to need a hose to connect your pressure washer to a water source. You're going to use the customer's water supply in order to complete the job. When it comes to hoses, you want to buy one that's 100 feet long and is heavy duty.

Anything less than 100 feet is going to become a hassle. You have no idea where the customer's water outlet is in relation to their car, so you need as much length as possible. You also want to go heavy duty here.

You want something that is going to last. You're going to be moving this hose from customer to customer. You're going to be stepping over it on a regular basis. It's also 100 feet long so a medium or light duty hose will easily get tangles and kinks in it that are no fun to stop what you're doing to deal with.

Trash Bags

Trash bags are something to easily overlook in your detailing business, but think about how you're cleaning out cars. There could be trash in the car that needs to be cleaned out or large pieces of debris that can't be picked up by your dry vac.

You need to throw this trash away somewhere, and you'll be ready to go by picking up some trash bags. The size you go with is really up to you because if you run out of space, you can always use another bag. So you could go with 4 gallon or 8 gallon trash bags and be fine in either case.

Wash and Wax

You need something to clean the surface of the exterior of the car with, and a wash and wax will be able to get the job done. It'll do a good job of getting the outside clean and leaving it with that nice and shiny finish.

Cleaner Degreaser

This is the type of solution that you want to use for cleaning the inside of someone's car. Over time, the center and front console can get dirty and grimy so you need something that can remove the grim and leave it looking new.

Glass cleaner

You'll want to use a specific cleaner for the glass windows of the car. You can usually buy this in a foam version or spray version. Either one works well, so buy both kinds to test them out and see which one you like more.

Tire shiner

Tire shiner is the product that's going to make those wheels look like they're brand new. It's a great service to provide as it can really enhance the overall look of the car's exterior. It's not even that expensive either; you can pick up a bottle for around $5-$7.

Spray Bottles

I recommend buying 2-3 spray bottles when you're starting out. This will allow you to put different solutions in each bottle that you need. For instance, you could mix up one spray bottle with your cleaner degreaser for the interior of the car.

You could use another spray bottle for your tire shiner, and you could use a third bottle for your glass cleaner. They're not very expensive; you're looking at a cost of around $3-$4 per bottle. You're always going to need them, so don't be afraid to start out with a few. It's not going to hurt anything if you bought 1 or 2 extras as you'll eventually find a use for them.

Detailing Brushes

When cleaning the wheels of a vehicle, you need a tool that can allow you to get into crevasses and thoroughly apply your solution to the tires. You also need brushes to clean the consoles that can get into the nooks and crannies without scratching the car. This is where soft detailing brushes will come into play. You can typically buy a pack of 5 brushes for around $10.

Leather Conditioner

Not every car you come across is going to be leather, but adding in leather conditioner is going to be a nice boost to your service. Some cars may have cloth seats but their steering wheel is made of leather, so you could still apply this product to the steering wheel. Leather conditioner will help to protect the leather from wearing down over time and it also smells great. You can get some good leather conditioner for around $15-$25 per bottle.

Buckets

You want to get a couple of 5 gallon buckets. This will allow you to mix up a good sized amount of your cleaning solution when cleaning the exterior of a car. You can easily and repeatedly dip your microfiber towel or wash mitt in the solution to keep things moving at a good pace.

Extension Cord

You're going to need an extension cord for your pressure washer, dry vac, and extractor. Similar to the garden hose, you're going to want to get a cord that's 100 feet in length. You don't know the conditions that you'll find yourself in, so it's better to play it safe and go for the longer cord. The price for a cord this long should only cost you around $25.

Three Prong Attachment

You have quite a few machines that need access to power. It's going to be super annoying to plug and unplug your extension cord from one device to the next depending on what you need to use at the time. By getting a three prong attachment for your extension cord, you can get all of your power supply devices plugged up at the same time. This makes it way more convenient to operate and allows you to seamlessly switch between your devices.

Microfiber Towels

You're going to need towels for every job that you do. Yes, these towels can be reused, but I recommend getting at least 30 towels and using them for different things. You might use one set of towels for the car's exterior, another set for the wheels, and your third set for the interior. You really can't have enough towels as a mobile detailer because you'll eventually use them!

Wash Mitt

You may prefer to wash a car's exterior with a wash mitt as opposed to a towel, but it's really up to your preference. A wash mitt isn't that expensive, so you can get one to try out and see how you like it in comparison to microfiber towels.

Adding It Up

If you added up the total cost of these supplies, you'd end up with a total of around $600-$700, depending on brands and where you live. That really isn't too bad! To think that you can start a business with life-changing potential for only $600-$700 is kind of crazy to think about.

You could go out and buy these supplies and be servicing your first client soon afterwards. A lot of different businesses that you could start can't do that. You also don't have to have any specific skills. You can get started with detailing cars and be good at it as long as you're thorough and don't rush through anything.

Getting Some Coverage

One other thing that I do recommend you look into is getting some business insurance. You want to look into getting some general liability insurance just because you are going to be working on people's cars, and cars are expensive. You could be dry vacuuming someone's car and you yank on the hose causing the dry vac to tip over and scratch the car.

You could forget to dilute your cleaning solution and it causes the dashboard to fade. There is a possibility of something going wrong, and since you're dealing with pricey cars, it's better to have coverage and the peace of mind that comes with it. A general liability insurance policy shouldn't cost that much, and it will be a good investment to make for your business.

The last thing you want is to operate your business always being too cautious because you're worried about what could go wrong. If you get some basic coverage, you don't have to worry about small little things that could go south, and that's priceless if you ask me.

Jump In Before You're Fully Ready

The last piece of advice I want to leave you with in this chapter is that ultimately, you're going to have to dive in and get started before you're fully ready. There's nothing that can fully prepare you for your first paying client. Yes, I recommend that you buy your supplies and get a general insurance policy.

I recommend that you detail your own car and practice on some of your friend's cars for free or heavily discounted to get some practice in. All the while, you should already be marketing your business. You need to start spreading the word because it may take a little bit of time to get your first client.

It might not, who knows? You just don't want to wait to start marketing because you don't feel like you're fully ready. You have to start spreading the word as soon as you possibly can.

If you're already getting people who are ready to book you, then you can schedule them a few days out. Spend those few days practicing if you don't feel comfortable jumping right into detailing a paying customer's car. I want you to understand that if you have feelings of doubt or apprehension, that is totally normal.

You have to embrace the fact that you're never going to feel 100% ready. You're going to stall out and try to think of other supplies that you might need. You might try to think of how you would handle every possible question that the customer might ask you, or how you would deal with x,y,z scenario.

All of those feelings are going to happen, so expect it, embrace it, and fight through it anyways. If you want to separate yourself from your competition, you have to think differently than they do. Remember the reasons why you're interested in starting this business in the first place. There's a reason why you're reading this book right now, so I want you to take that leap of faith even if you feel like you're not fully ready. The supplies I listed are more than enough to get you going, so don't let your mind talk you out of getting started!

Chapter 2: How to Get Customers for Your Car Detailing Business

You can buy the coolest supplies the market has to offer. You could even go all out and go ahead with purchasing that van and fully decking it out. You could tell your friends and family about how cool your van looks and post it on social media because you're so proud of it.

That's great, but you will get crushed every time by someone driving their own personal vehicle with the basic supplies needed who actually knows how to promote themselves. Supplies are an essential part of running a successful car detailing business without question, but none of that matters if you're not able to promote yourself in a way that gets people interested. It's kind of like buying furniture for a house you haven't even bought yet.

Yes, that home is going to need furniture, but the furniture is useless until you buy the home. It's the same type of premise with a car detailing business, which is why this chapter is going to be so important for you to closely pay attention to. I'm going to outline the tactics you need to follow to ensure that you can bring in clients and that your initial investment on supplies wasn't a waste of money.

Picture it Perfectly

I want you to visualize what type of vehicle you ideally want to work on. Do you want to work on anyone's car who's interested in your service? Or do you really enjoy high-end cars and that's the car you primarily want to work on?

You want to think about this step first because it's going to impact the way in which you market your business. If you want to work on motorcycles, your marketing strategy is going to be different from how you would market if you want to work on luxury vehicles. If you don't really care that much and just want to work on anyone's car who's willing to do business with you, then your marketing approach can be more general.

This isn't to say that you have to stick with one type of vehicle throughout the entirety of your business, but thinking about this ahead of time allows you to pull different marketing levers when needed. For instance, you could run a special specifically for motorcycles.

This promo could be more impactful than a general promo because it's going to speak directly to cyclists and have more of an impact on them. Therefore, they're going to be more likely to give you a call than if they just saw a general advertisement.

Build Your Online Presence

When it comes to marketing your mobile detailing business, I want you to start off with ways that are completely free and then work your way up to things that are more expensive. The first thing you can do to generate exposure for your business is to create a social media page for your business. This will allow you to easily get exposure as it doesn't cost anything to post on social media.

The first step to this is to actually post on your personal social media pages telling your followers about your detailing venture. The reason why you want to do this is because your personal profile already has followers. It doesn't matter how many followers your personal profile has.

It can be 100, 1,000, or 10,000. Anything is better than nothing. People who are already following your personal profile are likely doing so because they know who you are.

They're either your friend, family member, or an acquaintance you've met throughout life. These are going to be the first people you should tell about your business because they have the highest probability of becoming your first set of customers. These people already know who you are, so it's much easier to sell these people rather than someone who doesn't know you.

When you buy from someone you don't know, you're more thorough with your buying process. You'll check online reviews, you'll look at their website, you'll do everything you can to ensure their business is legit. When you're interacting with someone you know, you more or less skip to asking how much it's going to cost.

If the service is in your price range, you go ahead and sign up because you trust the person already. You could make a post along these lines on any personal profile that you have:

Hey everyone! I just wanted to give an update in my life to say that I'm starting a new business adventure that I'm very excited about! I've always loved cars ever since I was a kid, and anyone who knows me well knows that I love spending time keeping my own car looking nice and shiny. This is why I decided to start my own mobile detailing business. I come to you and handle everything to get your car looking fresh. I'm running a special promo for the launch of my business. If you're interested, send me a message with the word "car" and I'll get back to you asap.

A post like this could get you some clients right off the bat. It's an effective post for a lot of reasons. First, you're giving the reason why you're starting the business. You've always loved cars, so by working on them, you get to be around cars more, which makes sense.

It can be any reason as long as it is reasonable. Don't say something that sounds greedy such as, "I wanted to start this business to make a quick buck", or "I started this business so I could make some extra cash on the side." That's only going to turn people off because they don't want to fuel your frivolous endeavors.

If you haven't been a big car person, no worries; you could tell a story about how you got in your car one day and just thought about how unclean your car felt. So you detailed your car, and now it feels like you're getting into a new car every time. You want to help create that feeling for others, so you decided to start your own mobile detailing business.

Giving a reason for why you're starting the business gives people something they can hold on to. It makes them feel like they're not a dollar sign and that you're doing this to actually help them out. Secondly, you're mentioning that you're a mobile service, which lets people know that your service is convenient.

They don't have to worry about logistics or driving to a place that's far away. You're letting them know that it's going to be easy to get the service done. Thirdly, you tell them about a promo and give them specific instructions for how to take advantage of it.

They message you the word "car" and you take it from there. They don't have to think about what message to send you because you've taken the guesswork out of the equation. You'll also notice that you're not mentioning a price in your post.

There's a very important reason for this, so stay tuned. Finally, you can make this post even more effective by adding before and after photos. You can use your own car for this, especially if you're using it as part of your story for why you started this business in the first place.

What Else Should You Post About?

You don't want to make one post and then abandon social media. It's a great tool that can continually bring you leads when used correctly. With social media, you really get out of it what you put into it.

If you only post once per week or every two weeks, then you're not going to see too many results from it. Before anything else, you need to decide how many times per week you want to post. The most important factor is choosing an amount that you can actually keep up with. Don't tell yourself that you're going to post twice a day when realistically you can only post five times per week. It's better to be honest with yourself and be consistent five times per week. Once you have your frequency down, here are some things you can post about:

Cleaning Cars

A lot of social media platforms offer the ability to post stories, which are short clips of videos or pictures you can post that disappear after 24 hours. You can post stories of you working on cars. It can be short action shots of you spraying a car down or dry vacuuming a car's interior.

You could also post before and after photos on your story as well. Posting yourself cleaning cars is a good idea because it's good social proof. You're showing your followers that their peers are getting their cars cleaned, and it will make others feel inclined to do the same.

The Products You Use

You can also make posts about the various products you use and why they're so effective. These kinds of posts will help to demonstrate your knowledge about cars to your audience.

How You Remove Stains or Other Parts of the Cleaning Process

You can show people on your social media how you get rid of stains on the seats or floorboards. You can show them how you clean up tight areas. You can let them know the steps you take when cleaning the outside of the car and lots more.

Post a Before and After of Every Car You Detail

Every car that you service, you should post a before and after of the car. Again, this is similar to posting on the job because it's social proof.

You're showing other people that someone got their car cleaned. "If you want your car to look like this person's, then you should definitely give me a call." The more before and after pictures you post, the better off you'll be because you're building more and more trust with your followers.

Print Flyers

The next step you need to take after your online presence is squared away is to print some flyers. This isn't free like social media, but the price isn't going to be too expensive. This is especially true considering that these flyers can help generate a lot of business for you.

What you want to do with these flyers is place them on the windshields of cars. Anyone who has a car could potentially be a customer, but you can be a little targeted with it if need be. For example, if you come across an older car, the owner might care less about the appearance of their vehicle compared to someone with a newer car.

You don't want to make any assumptions, but you only have so many flyers you can put on cars. Every single flyer that you use is going to cost you money. Therefore, you need to be strategic with every car you put a flyer on.

Newer cars or luxury cars are going to give you a better chance of getting a call because these car owners likely have more invested in their car. They're going to be willing to spend more money to keep it looking nice. I recommend only printing off a couple hundred flyers in the beginning.

The reason being is that you don't have your website set up yet. You still want to get some flyers printed because it's going to take a while for your website to be created. You don't want to sit around waiting when you could have already printed off some flyers and had them generate some customers for you.

Initially, you can just put your business name, email, phone number, and social media channels on your first batch of flyers. Get them printed and start passing them out. In the meantime, you can start to work on your website.

Building Your Online Presence Part 2

The first part to building your online presence is going to involve getting your social media channels up and running. The second part is going to involve creating your own website. Having a website isn't a necessity, but it can help to build a lot of trust in this day and age.

People are expecting you to have a website for your business. Are your friends and family going to care if you have a website? Probably not. You can certainly detail your inner circle's cars and rely on word of mouth to build your business, in which case you wouldn't have to rely much on a website.

However, having a website is only going to help you convert interested prospects into paying customers. You want to be sure that your website includes plenty of the cars you've cleaned so that people can see firsthand the type of work that you do. Include pictures of a car's interior and exterior.

Include close ups of certain areas like the center console if it was really dirty and grimy. A general picture of the interior might not do it justice, but a close up definitely will. Also include a contact section where people can get more information about your service and schedule a time for the detail.

Also include a biography section where you talk about who you are as a person, what your interests are, and how you came to start this business. These are the main things you want to consider when you or someone else is building your website. I want you to think about other mobile detailers that you're going to be competing with in your area.

They might not be willing to spend the money to create a website. I encourage you to think differently than your competitors. Imagine someone is interested in a mobile detailing service so they do an online search for "mobile car detailer near me."

Your business can actually pop up in the search results because you have a website. That's a job you can land purely because you were willing to go the extra mile and make that investment. Also picture someone hearing about your business and rushing to try to find you online, but they can't because you don't have a website. You don't want to miss out on potential customers because you weren't willing to create a website.

Car Dealerships

You can also go to various car dealerships in your area and pitch your service to them. You can get a contract to work on some of their cars to make sure they look super spiffy for sale. You can negotiate a rate with them, but due to the volume they can supply you, you typically won't make as much per car. However, it is something to consider if you run into a dry spell with getting customers.

Offer a Rewards Program

Once you get a customer, you want to incentivize them to use your business time and time again. A good way to achieve that is by offering a free service every so often. For instance, you could say that you get your 10th detail for free.

You could easily keep track of this using a business card or flyer and stamping the date of each service that is performed on it. Or you could simply sign off on the card. You could use a hole punch, but people might just hole punch the card some themselves to get closer to the free service.

If you want to use a method like hold punching, I recommend you keep track of customers separately in a spreadsheet. This way you can tell if the number of holes in the card matches up with what your spreadsheet is telling you. This is a common practice you'll see places like ice cream shops or dry cleaners do, and it can work great for your car detailing business.

It's so effective because as people start to get closer to that 10th time, they'll psychologically want to use your service as often as possible because they're working towards a goal. Once they get that free service, it will feel like they achieved that goal. You might be hesitant to implement this idea because it will involve you giving away a free service every so often.

I can understand why you might feel that way, but you're actually making money because you're incentivizing people to get their car detailed with you over anyone else first and foremost. Secondly, you're incentivizing people to use your service when they normally wouldn't have. You only give out the free service if they get to their 10th detail, so the customer has more than made up for that free detail if they have already used you nine times previously.

Run Specials

You can run a special if you hit a dry patch in your business and you need to drum up some interest. You can also run a special for any type of holiday, your birthday, or the anniversary date for when you started the business. Yes, you will be giving customers a discount from your normal rate, but it's all about perspective.

These people might not have booked you for a detail at your regular rate. You might not be maximizing your profits, but it can be a good way to get people to try out your service. Once they try it out and realize how good you are, you can rely on your rewards program to keep them coming back for more.

If you really knock their socks off, they'll tell their friends about your business. This will definitely happen if you make their car look so good that their friends can't help but to ask how they got their car to look that way. So think futuristically and don't worry about the initial loss.

Think of it more like a free sample. When a company gives away a free sample of let's say laundry detergent, yes they're losing money up front. The goal is to get customers to try the product and if they like it, they'll continue to buy that detergent for months and years to come, so the sample is really a small price to pay.

That's the mentality I want you to have when it comes to running promos. It's not going to be practical to run a promo year-round, so you want to be strategic with when you use them.

How to Run a Promo Effectively

The first step to running an effective promo is to have a reason for running the promo. Running a promotion just because can seem sporadic and create skepticism with your followers. It can make you seem desperate for business. This is why you want to come up with a reason for the promo, which can be anything really.

If you need to run a promotion right now, it's easier to find a reason for it rather than wait for a more legitimate reason such as your birthday. A couple of examples could be that you started your business on the 16th of the month so you're running a special, or you started your business on a Friday, so you're running a special. It could be national boyfriend day, so you run a special so your boyfriend can finally get his car cleaned.

It could be national dog day, so you run a special for people to finally get all of that pet hair from their beloved pet cleaned up. You could run a special for being in business for six months, three months, or even one month. There are no rules to this, but having a reason is going to be better than not having a reason.

The next step to running an effective special is to give people a reason to participate. You can do this by giving away a free car detail for one person. If you offer different packages such as a full detail and full exterior wash, you could give away one free detail for each of the different packages that you offer.

For example, you could have people send you pictures of their car and the winners are the cars that you deem to be in the most dire need of some help. You could also have people leave a comment with how long it's been since they've last cleaned their car and the winner could be the person who's gone the longest without cleaning their car. This is an effective way to approach things because the comments will show engagement, which will make the algorithm show your post to more people.

You could also have people comment as to why they should win the free detail. You could have people guess a number between one and 100 and comment their answer. You could have people comment a caption to a car related picture and the funniest caption wins.

You could have people guess how many gallons on average it takes to wash a car and the closest answer wins. There are tons of different approaches to this, and you can switch it up every time you run a promo. No matter which way you choose to go about it, this step cannot be missed as it's the single biggest factor to having a successful special.

It may sound silly, but it gets people invested in what you're offering. If you skip this step, people might see your promo and just gloss over it. If they know they have a chance to win something of value for free, they'll participate and be invested to see if they won.

The reality is that most people who participate won't win, but now they might be more interested in getting their car detailed from you compared to before they participated in the special. Finally, make sure you run the promo over a few days and post about it every single day. Let's say you want to run a special for your birthday on October 20th.

You don't want to wait until October 20th to tell people about the promo and then have it end that same day. Instead, you want to tell people about the promo a few days before, start the promo on October 20th, and then let it run for a few days before ending it. Doing things in this manner will give people plenty of opportunities to take advantage of the promo.

If you only tell people the day of and it ends that same day, there will be some people who don't even see the post until the next day; at this point, it's already too late. You don't want your followers to potentially get irritated with you because you didn't go about things the right way. Here's how you can introduce the promo a couple of days before it actually happens:

"Hey everyone! As you may or may not know, two days from now is my 28th birthday. I don't want to be the only one celebrating, so I want to give you something to celebrate as well. I'm going to do a giveaway for a free full interior and exterior detail for the winner. On that day, anyone who wishes me a happy birthday in the comment section on that post will be entered into a raffle to win the free detail. Even if you don't win, there's still reason to cheer as all participants will receive a coupon for 15% off of their next detail. The giveaway post will happen on my birthday October 20th, and you'll have until October 22nd at midnight to enter the giveaway, if you're interested. Cheers!"

Then on the actual day of your birthday, you can make the official giveaway post where you'll essentially reiterate details from your previous post:

"As I mentioned in my last post, today is my birthday and I want to celebrate it with you! Comment down below, and you'll be entered into the raffle. The winner will receive a free full interior and exterior car detail. All participants will receive 15% off of a car detail. The contest will end October 22nd at midnight. Best of luck!"

And then on the last day of the contest, you want to remind people that the giveaway will be closing and that today is the last day to enter the contest.

"Hey everyone! It's a couple of days past my birthday, but I want to keep the party going! Just as a reminder, today is the last day to enter in the giveaway for the free detail. You can still participate and receive a coupon, even if you don't win. The giveaway will end tonight at midnight, and I'll announce the winner tomorrow at 5 PM."

Once you announce the winner, your job is not done yet. Anyone who entered into the contest is interested in your service or else they wouldn't have participated in the giveaway. Those are hot leads, and you need to go and seal the deal!

Don't just let them sit there and go cold. Simply reach out and message every person who participated individually to ask if they prefer to receive their coupon via email or via message on whatever social media platform you're using. Once they answer, you can say something along the lines of, "Okay great! When would be a good time to schedule? I have a full day open on Thursday."

Saying this might sound a bit pushy, but you'll be surprised by the response you get. Worst case scenario, someone will say that they'll reach out to you when they're ready. A lot of times though, they'll start trying to figure out a good time.

Sometimes you really just have to go for it. If sending a message like that feels out of your comfort zone, then you can simply say this instead, "Okay awesome! I have some openings next week so feel free to book a time whenever!" This is a much softer approach and leaves the ball in the customer's court.

They'll usually respond with something like, "sounds good" or "okay will do." Sometimes though, they will start chatting about setting up a time for a detail. Whatever your approach is, you have to open that door.

You're leaving money on the table if you're waiting for people to reach out to you. Yes, some people definitely will reach out on their own, but you're going to see much more success when you reach out and do your best to make it happen!

Offer Subscription Packages

Another thing you can offer are subscriptions to your detailing business. For instance, when someone signs up they pay a monthly rate for a detail. Then they get charged that amount every single month no matter what.

It doesn't matter if they get their car detailed that month or not. Of course, you'll want to incentivize people to want to sign up for your monthly subscription. You can do this by offering a 10% discount off from your normal rate.

This works out great for people who know that they want to get their car detailed consistently. One thing you need to consider when doing a subscription is what you should do if they pay for a detail but don't get around to using it that month. Do you roll over that credit, or is it just too bad for the customer?

My recommendation is that you do rollover credits that aren't used by the customer. This way no one is going to be upset if they had a month where they weren't able to get around to using your service. It's also unlikely that they'll get around to using their extra credits because this would mean that they'd be getting their car detailed multiple times in the same month.

Someone could definitely use your service on a bi-weekly basis to use up their extra credits, but the good news for you is that their car shouldn't be in too bad of shape because you just detailed it recently. More than likely though, they won't get around to using their extra credits, but you're still going to make money from the subscription.

Subscriptions are great because it's guaranteed revenue for your business. This is income that you can count on every single month no matter what. This is why it's absolutely worth giving someone a 10% discount from your normal rate.

In recent times, lots of different businesses have started to offer subscriptions for their services such as car washes and movie theaters. A movie theater might offer unlimited movies and discounts at the concession stand, and they'll charge $20 per month for the subscription. This means you'd have to see at least 2 movies per month to break even for your subscription.

It also ensures that you come to the movie theater because you don't want your subscription to go to waste. Now that you're at the movie theater, you're going to get some snacks and a drink at the concession stand, especially considering that you get a discount. The concession stand is where the real money is made for movie theaters, so every time you show up to the theater, you're going to go to the concession stand.

This is why offering a subscription is a win for the theater. If you don't see any movies for the month, they're still making money. If you see every movie that comes out, you're likely going to come to the concession stand, and they'll still make money.

You'd have to see every movie and not go to the concession stand in order for it to not be worth it from the company's perspective, which is unlikely. It's a similar type of premise with your car detailing business; you're going to be making money from someone that month regardless of if they use your service or not. This is why I think it's a great offer to include in your business.

What Should You Charge?

Determining your pricing can be one of the most stressful aspects of your business. Pricing alone can make you delay starting your business. You can sit there and worry that you're charging too much and that no one will want to use your service, so you come up with a lower price point.

Then you start to think, "Is this business even worth it? I'm barely going to make any money at this rate!" I don't want you to have this constant back and forth battle with yourself about your rate. So in this section, I'm going to break down some factors you can use to determine a rate that you feel comfortable with.

It All Depends

When it comes to car detailing, no two jobs are the same. This is the first thing you have to take into consideration. This means you're not going to charge the same flat rate every single time no matter what.

That would not be a good move on your part. Think about it. Cars come in different sizes for starters.

A big diesel truck is not the same as a compact car. Why should a compact car be priced the same as a big truck? It's going to take you more time to clean the truck because it's simply bigger.

The next thing you have to think about is the condition of the car. A compact car may be smaller than a truck, but what if it's absolutely disgusting and the truck isn't too bad? Well, now it's going to take a longer time to clean the compact car than the truck due to its terrible condition.

If you charge a flat rate, you're doing yourself no favors because it's going to take you way longer to service that vehicle. This is why you shouldn't list your prices online. You can't give a flat rate and expect it to be the same for everyone's vehicle that you service.

You need the customer to send you pictures of the current state of their car. You also need to know what kind of vehicle they have. Once you have the right information, then you can properly assess how much you should charge them.

Getting pictures before you give them a quote may seem like a hassle, but it will pay off. You're handling potential issues ahead of time, which is far better than getting to the job and telling the customer you're going to charge them more from what you originally told them. Even though the price works itself out to the same thing, the way it's delivered to the customer is completely different.

People don't like being told one price just for things to change on them. Yes, the condition of the car is the reason for the price increase, but some people aren't going to be understanding of that. They'll think that's what they're paying you for in the first place is to clean their car, so why should more money be tacked on?

As a business owner, you fully understand why more money needs to be added. This car is going to take you a longer time, and that's time you could be spending on another car. It boils down to you missing out on money if you charge this person the same normal rate.

What if this was a truck that went mudding and it's completely caked in mud on the outside and the floorboards are covered in mud as well? By understanding the scope of the job ahead of time, the customer won't know they're getting charged extra because of the condition of the car.

You'll name your price, and they'll either agree or they won't. They might ask you why the price is what it is, and in that case you can mention the condition the car is in.

How Much Should Someone Pay You?

So when push comes to shove, what should your general rate be for a full-service car detail? Well, on the low end of things, I say you shouldn't go below $100. You should only consider a price point of around $100 if you want to be competitive in the market and your pricing is the way in which you want to compete.

On the high end of things, you could charge around $200. When you're starting out, this may be too high of a price point to go with as you're not an established business yet. You don't have reviews, and it's going to be harder to get clients.

You're not going to have as many people reaching out to you like other companies might. Competition is also a big factor in what you should initially charge. If you have some established detailers in your area that are charging $200 for a full-service detail, then I wouldn't advise you to charge $200 for your service.

You're going to have a hard time getting people to go with your detailing company over the competition. I'd start off in the realm of $125-$150 for a full-service detail. So as a baseline example, I might charge $125 for cars, $135 for SUVs, and $150 for vehicles with three rows of seats or half ton trucks.

This way my initial baseline pricing takes the size of the vehicle into consideration. Next, you'd want to factor in the condition. This is more subjective, but it can help to think about how much longer you think the job is going to take because of the condition and then adjust your price accordingly.

Let's say a normal full-scale detail takes you three hours on average. You estimate this car is going to take you four hours based on how dirty it is. It's a full-size car, so the normal rate is $125 or about $42 an hour. You'd add in an extra $42 to make up for that extra hour you're going to spend cleaning the car.

Offer Different Packages

You definitely want to have a full-service detail option for people, but you should consider different package options that people can buy. This will help you appeal to a wider range of people. Someone might not need or want a full interior cleaning, but they might want an exterior cleaning.

If you only offer a full-service package, then this is business that you could miss out on. You could offer a full exterior package such as a wash and wax and tire clean and shine. You could charge roughly 40% of what you do for the full-service package.

So a car would be $50, $54 for SUVs, and $60 for three rows of seats or half ton and up trucks. From there, you would then increase the price if the car is really dirty based on how much extra time you think it would take you. You can offer more than two different packages, but in the beginning, I recommend that you keep it simple and stick to something like I mentioned with these two packages.

Sometimes too many options actually has the opposite of the intended effect. It creates too much overwhelm for the customer to decide, so they end up doing nothing at all. With two choices, you're keeping things simple, and it's very easy for someone to make a decision for what they need.

Should You Factor in Gas?

Since you're a mobile detailer, you're going to be driving all over the place. It's going to cost you money to go from customer to customer. So should you make the customer pay for your trip in the form of a gas charge?

Well, I would say probably not up to a certain point. Your gas costs should already be factored into your baseline pricing. It feels wrong to tack that on and have that burden on the customer when mobile is their only option to do business with you.

It's not like you have a physical location where they could choose to come in if they wanted to save money on the gas charge. This has limits though. You're going to spend way more in gas going to a customer that's an hour away vs. 10 minutes away.

So how do you handle this? It's your business, and you get to ultimately decide what's within your limits and what isn't. This also depends on what kind of car you're driving.

Your car might get great gas mileage. If that's the case, you may not feel the need to implement a gas charge at all. Conversely, your current vehicle might not get the best gas mileage, so you're thinking you definitely want to include a gas charge for customers who are a certain distance or greater from you. You need to establish your limits first.

What's the furthest you're willing to go to detail a car? An hour is a pretty reasonable limit. Now you need to decide at what point you want to tack on a gas charge to your price.

You could implement a charge for any location that's at least 30 minutes away. From there, you could increase your charge incrementally based on the distance. For example, a 30-minute drive could incur a gas charge of $10.

A 45-minute drive could incur a charge of $15 and $20 if the drive is an hour long. You could keep things simple like that if you want to, or you could calculate it out to get more precise. You could charge something such as $0.55 per mile, and then charge that amount for every mile that's over your baseline limit.

Chapter 3: Some Things to Think About When You're Detailing Cars

The idea of cleaning and detailing a car seems simple enough. However, there are some nuances that you might not be thinking about. In this chapter, I want to go over some of those mistakes so that your first few jobs go smoothly and you don't find yourself in an awkward situation with a customer.

Understand What They're Expecting

Before you even start on a job, you need to understand what the customer is expecting from you. This can help to solve issues before they even arise. What you think is realistic could be totally different from what the customer thinks is realistic. You're the professional, so you're going to have realistic expectations for what can be achieved and what can't be.

The customer might not have a good understanding of what can be accomplished.

Let's say the customer has a coffee stain on their passenger seat that's three years old. The customer might be expecting you to completely remove the stain and restore it to a status that looks close to like new.

You can't assume that the customer is going to be understanding if you're unable to completely remove the stains. Therefore, it's a good idea to talk about expectations during the booking process. It doesn't matter if you're talking with someone on the phone, email, or direct message.

Ask the customer what their expectations are for the service or specifically point out things that might cause a potential issue. For example, if you see loose debris on the floorboard, you don't have to call that out because you know you'll easily be able to remove that with a dry vac. If a customer sends you a picture of their seats and you see a stain on one of them, ask if they know how long the stain has been there.

Then you can proceed to tell the customer that the longer a stain has been on the seat, the less chance there is of it coming completely out. You might be able to get the stain to lighten up, but you can't guarantee that the stain will come out 100%. I learned to do this from my days of cleaning mattresses.

I would say this to customers, and it would work great. You could set the expectation clearly beforehand so that way you and the customer are on the same page and there's no pressure to remove a stain completely if you're not able to. Before I started doing this, customers would sometimes get upset because their mattress wasn't coming back looking pearly white.

They didn't care that the stains lightened up because they were thinking it was going to look like it was brand new. Things went a lot better when I would talk about what they were expecting before I started working on their mattress, and this works just as well when it comes to cleaning cars. So if you have a concern about anything you see, don't hesitate to address it before you start the job.

Get Everything Set Up Before You Start

I recommend getting all of your supplies set up and ready before you officially do anything. Get out your pressure washer, extractor, dry vac, garden hose, extension cord, buckets, and solution. Then mix up your cleaning solution in your bucket.

Get your extension cord and water hose plugged up. Use your three prong attachment and get your dry vac and extractor plugged up. Initially, when you're cleaning the car's exterior, you're only going to need the pressure washer, but this allows you to quickly switch between devices without having to stop what you're doing to get a different machine set up.

I like doing things in this manner because it allows you to continue working without breaking your flow. Once you get into a groove, you can keep it moving if everything is set up prior to you starting. Imagine dry vacuuming a car then having to stop to get your extractor set up before you can get to removing stains. It's far easier to dry vac and then immediately move into extracting because you did the prep work ahead of time.

Wear Disposable Gloves

Yes, wearing gloves is going to be another expense you're going to incur. The good news is that disposable gloves aren't that expensive, and the benefit they provide to you is well worth the cost and the hassle of putting them on. The reason why you want to wear gloves is because you're going to be dealing with a lot of chemicals on a daily basis.

These chemicals can dry out your hands as the day goes on. Secondly, you don't know what you're going to come across on the inside of someone's car. You're going to be dealing with some trash and potentially other disgusting stains and debris.

With gloves, you can easily pick up any trash without the worry of it being sticky, grimy, or gross. By wearing disposable gloves, you can easily switch into a new pair if you come across something gross that makes you need to change your gloves. You don't want to get something on your gloves only for it to get onto a part of the car you just cleaned. Backtracking is no fun, so I recommend getting a box of 100 disposable gloves to have on you at jobs so that you're ready for whatever comes your way!

Dilute Your Cleaning Solutions

Whenever you buy a cleaning solution, it's very concentrated. It's not meant to be used directly on a surface as is. You need to dilute your cleaning solutions before you use them, which you can do using water.

Luckily, you don't have to worry about guessing if you're diluting with the correct amount of water. On the back of the product, it will tell you how much to dilute the solution. For instance, it might be something like eight parts water to one part solution or 10 parts water to one part solution.

So let's say your cleaning solution calls for eight parts water to one part solution, and you need to make ½ gallon of your cleaning solution. Your cleaning solution is going to be 64 fluid ounces in total. 57 of those 64 ounces are going to be water and the remaining seven are going to be the cleaning solution.

Refill Your Bottles at the End of Every Job

Another pro tip is to refill your spray bottles at the end of every job. If you're leaving a job to go home, you're not going to feel like refilling them when you get home. You're going to forget about it, and then when you get to your next job, you're going to be upset at the extra prep work you have to do.

If you're going from one job straight to the next, then you're already setting yourself up for success by having less prep work to do at the start. Refilling your bottles makes it less likely that you're going to have to stop in the middle of a job because you need to mix up more of a certain cleaning solution. It kind of reminds me of mowing the grass for the first time when spring rolls around before it gets too out of hand.

I'm usually a little bit lazier than I should be when mowing for the first time after winter. When I wait and the grass grows up, it's harder for my mower to get through the grass. If I would just mow sooner, it would be a lot easier to cut through the grass.

It's the same way with mobile detailing. I hate being in the middle of something only to run out of a solution and have to stop what I'm doing to make more. It just ruins the flow of things.

Clean the Cars Exterior in a Pattern

When you're cleaning the exterior of a car, you first and foremost want to make sure that you're spraying the car with your pressure washer starting at the top and working your way down. If you go from the bottom up, you're basically going to have to go over the car multiple times because the dust and dirt from the top of the car will slide down towards the bottom. If you clean the bottom first, it's just going to get dirty again once you clean the top.

By going top down, you ensure the dirt slides down until it's off the car without having to backtrack. Make sure you come up with a pattern when cleaning to ensure you're not cleaning the same area of a car multiple times. You don't want to be wasting time when you could be servicing more customers. Lastly, don't forget to clean the door jam!

Ask the Customer if They're Satisfied

Once you finish the job, don't just tell the customer you're done and then try to hurry up and leave. Ask them to take a look at the vehicle to see if they're 100% satisfied with how their car looks. Have them take a good look at both the outside and inside. If they do have any issues, do what you can to correct the issue or issues that they have.

Maybe there was something you skipped over or missed on accident. By letting the customer look things over, they might notice something you missed. If they point out something such as a stain on a cushion not coming out, you could explain that you were able to lighten up the stain but it was too settled to remove completely.

Whatever the scenario is, this could save you from receiving a negative review. It's going to be unlikely that a customer tells you they were 100% satisfied and then leave a negative review. This would be contradictory behavior from what they told you after you finished the job, so it's unlikely to happen. What is more likely to happen is that the customer will leave you a positive review because you're leaving that job knowing that the customer was happy with your work.

Chapter 4: Bringing on a Teammate

As you begin to grow your business, you're going to start to find that you are your own biggest bottle neck. This isn't a knock on you; it's just the reality of the situation. You are only one person, and you can only do so much. Not only that but cleaning cars week after week can really be exhausting at times. In this chapter, you'll learn when you should consider bringing on someone who can help you detail cars and how to work with them effectively.

When Will You Need Extra Help with Your Detailing Business?

Initially, you're not going to have enough customers to justify having someone help you out. Yes, it might be nice, but you're going to have to pay that person. It's only going to eat into your profit margins for a job you could've handled on your own. If you're able to comfortably handle the amount of detailing gigs you're currently getting, then it's not time to bring on a helper. Once you start missing out on jobs because your schedule is full and you still have people calling you, that's when you want to start looking for additional help.

How Should You Use This Extra Helper?

There's really a couple of different ways you could use the extra help. The first way is to have the person complete jobs separately on their own. You need to supply them with the necessary materials, and this could allow you to schedule appointments at times you otherwise wouldn't be able to.

For instance, you might have two customers who live far apart, and both are only able to schedule at 11:00 A.M. By setting things up in this manner, you could service both people at the same time. The other way to go about things is to have the person work alongside you on the same job so that it's completed at a faster rate.

I personally like the route of having the person work alongside you better. The reason is that this is going to be a new person that you'll need to thoroughly train regardless. Even if you wanted to go about things where they complete jobs separately, they'd still have to spend a period of time training under your wing.

You need to make sure that they can do things properly before they do details on their own. Even with extensive training, how can you ensure the job is being done correctly once you're out of sight? The person might cut corners to get jobs done faster because they might not pay attention to small nuances like you do.

You won't know until you get a complaint from a customer, which means the damage has already been done. When someone works alongside you, they're always held accountable, and you can ensure that they're doing quality work every single time. You also don't have to spend extra money on an extra set of supplies.

Where to Find Help?

I recommend that you look to people you know or acquaintances to try to find a good fit. You can trust someone you already know more easily than a complete stranger. Reach out to anyone you think might be a good fit. If no one comes to mind or you're not able to find anyone who's interested, then you can post on your personal social media page to get someone to respond:

"As you may or may not know, I run my own car detailing business. Things have been picking up lately, and I'm looking for some part time help to assist me with some of the jobs that I'm doing. Starting pay is $15 per hour, and you can start as early as next week. If you're interested, send me a message saying "fresh and clean" and I'll get back to you as soon as I can."

You're increasing the effectiveness of this post by letting people know how much you're willing to pay. It's up to you to decide how much you're willing to pay, and this can depend a lot based on where you live. By being upfront with your pay, you can incentivize a lot of people to reach out right from the jump.

Letting people know that you're looking to quickly bring someone on and have them start next week helps as well. The more you're willing to offer pay wise, the more people you're going to have reach out, but you don't want it to eat into your profits too much, so think of a number you think is fair.

What if You Don't Get Any Good Leads?

If you don't get any good leads from your social media post, then consider looking at online groups for your local area to see if you can find anyone. You could post in local detail or car groups. If someone likes cars, chances are they already take good care of their car, and they'd be able to do the same for other people's cars as well. You could also post about your opening to community groups for your neighborhood. These are all free ways that you can look for an extra set of hands to help you out.

As we reach the end of this book, I'd like to ask for a small favor. Would you mind taking a minute and leaving a review for this book? I worked really hard to put this guide together and I'll gladly read over what you have to say!

Conclusion

The thing I love most about a car detailing business is how quickly you can get things up and going. You can get your first client pretty quickly with just a little bit of hustle, and before you know it, you'll have paid off all of your initial supplies. After reading this book, there really isn't anything that can stop you from succeeding as long as you don't get in your own way.

Even with good knowledge, it can still be tempting to do things that you shouldn't. You might be tempted to want to go all out with your supplies and deck out a van, but I need you to resist that urge at first. Focusing on lead generation is going to be much more beneficial.

You might be doubting if you're able to do this type of work, and if you're going to be able to leave customers with a service they'll be happy with. I'm here to tell you that you can absolutely pull this off if you believe in yourself and are willing to go the extra mile when others want to give up.

A lot of times, it only takes one customer to go from doubting everything to believing that you can do this. So don't give up because success could be right around the corner for you.